Animals
of North America

by Joy Nolan

Table of Contents

Introduction 2

Chapter 1 Animals and
Their Habitats 4

Chapter 2 All Kinds of Animals 14

Chapter 3 Changing Habitats 22

Conclusion 28

Solve This Answers 30

Glossary 31

Index 32

Introduction

Birds flap their wings to fly through the air. Fish have fins and tails that help them swim. Animals move, eat, breathe, and live in different ways. And they all have what they need to **survive** (ser-VIVE).

Animals have lived in many different places, or **habitats** (HA-bih-tats), in North America for millions of years.

Each animal **species** ▲ (SPEE-sheez) has features that help it survive in its habitat.

▲ The Apatosaurus (uh-pa-tuh-SOR-us) lived in North America about 150 million years ago. Its long neck helped it reach into forests to eat from trees.

Find out how animals stay alive in their habitats. Learn about some animals that are now **extinct** (ik-STINGKT). Many more animals could die out unless they are kept safe.

Animals and Their Habitats

North America is a huge **continent** (KAHN-tih-nent). It reaches up toward the icy North Pole. It stretches down toward the steamy **equator** (ih-KWAY-ter). North America has many animal habitats. Which is closest to where you live?

There are animals in the forests and deserts of North America. The grasslands, prairies, and mountains are home to animals, too. And there are animals in our lakes, rivers, and oceans. Each habitat provides food, water, air, and shelter to the animals there. Let's visit some habitats for a closer look.

1 SOLVE THIS

Use the map on page 5 to solve the following problems.
a. Which North American habitat is the biggest?
b. Which North American habitat is the smallest?
c. Which two habitats are farthest from each other?

Math Point

What steps did you follow to solve the problems?

4

HABITATS OF NORTH AMERICA

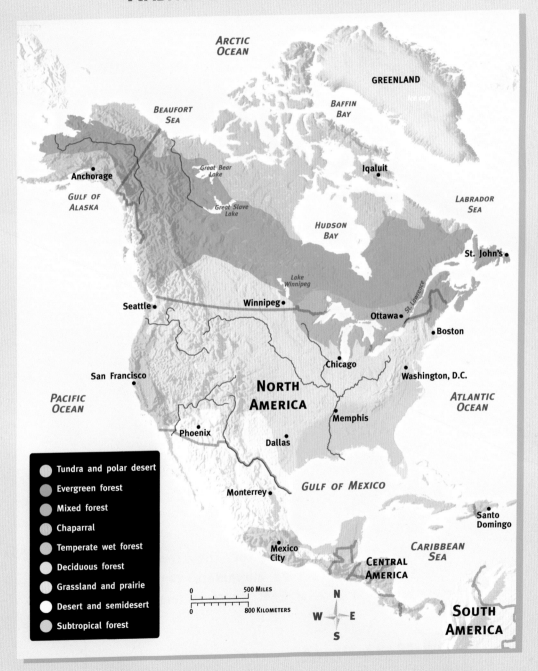

ARCTIC OCEAN

GREENLAND

BEAUFORT SEA

BAFFIN BAY

Anchorage

Great Bear Lake

Iqaluit

GULF OF ALASKA

LABRADOR SEA

Great Slave Lake

HUDSON BAY

St. John's

Lake Winnipeg

St. Lawrence

Seattle

Winnipeg

Ottawa

Boston

Chicago

San Francisco

Washington, D.C.

PACIFIC OCEAN

NORTH AMERICA

ATLANTIC OCEAN

Memphis

Phoenix

Dallas

Monterrey

GULF OF MEXICO

Santo Domingo

CARIBBEAN SEA

Mexico City

CENTRAL AMERICA

SOUTH AMERICA

Tundra and polar desert

Evergreen forest

Mixed forest

Chaparral

Temperate wet forest

Deciduous forest

Grassland and prairie

Desert and semidesert

Subtropical forest

0   500 MILES
0   800 KILOMETERS

N
W   E
S

5

Polar Deserts and Other Cold Places

The polar bear lives in the Arctic (ARK-tik). It's too cold for trees and most plants to grow there. The bear's fur and body fat keep it warm. Its padded paws help it to walk on the ice. The polar bear is a good swimmer. It makes catching a seal for dinner look easy.

2 SOLVE THIS

Polar bears move around a lot. They can travel about 15 miles (about 24 kilometers) per day. How far could a polar bear travel in one week?

 Math Point

Did it help to estimate your answer?

Moose, foxes, snowshoe rabbits, and great horned owls live in cold areas. Evergreen trees, which stay green all year, are found here.

▲ The arctic fox is well **camouflaged** (KA-muh-flahjd), or hidden. It has a dark coat of fur in spring and summer, which matches the earth. In winter its warm fur turns white and matches the snow.

▲ The musk ox and the snowshoe rabbit have broad feet that help them walk in deep snow.

IT'S A FACT

People in cold places sometimes find bones and other fossils (FAH-sulz) of woolly mammoths when they dig to build houses or roads. The frozen ground is like a refrigerator. It keeps body parts from falling apart.

▲ The woolly mammoth lived during the Ice Age, about 10,000 years ago. Its thick fur and body fat kept it warm.

All Kinds of Forests

Some forests have both evergreen trees and trees that lose leaves in the fall. Black bears, beavers, deer, and ducks live in forests. Toads and frogs live in forests, too.

▲ black bear

Everyday SCIENCE

Beware of the Bear!
Black bears are a problem in some areas. Here's what wildlife experts (EK-sperts) say about keeping safe from bears:
- Never feed bears.
- Only put out birdfeeders in the winter when bears **hibernate** (HY-ber-nate).
- Keep garbage cans in a safe place.
- When camping, always store food properly.

▲ beavers

▲ Salamanders like cool temperatures and lots of rain.

Deserts and Other Warm Places

It is hot and dry in the desert, and it may not rain for months. Animals that like it here are bighorn sheep, rabbits, coyotes (ky-OH-teez), desert tortoises (TOR-tus-ez), and armadillos (ar-muh-DIH-loze). Lizards, snakes, and many insects live here, too.

◀ The jack rabbit's big, flat ears help to keep it cool in the desert heat.

3 SOLVE THIS

It can be about about 123° Fahrenheit during the day in the desert. Nights, however, can be 30° to 50°F colder. If the daytime temperature is 123°F, what is the nighttime temperature range?

✓ Math Point

What information did you need to solve the problem?

▲ Armadillos dig into the ground to stay cool and to find bugs to eat.

▲ The coyote and other desert animals are **nocturnal** (nahk-TER-nul). They are more active at night when it's cooler.

Thick, short evergreen shrubs that cover the ground are called chaparral (sha-puh-RAL). Animals that commonly live in and around chaparral are coyotes, brush rabbits, mountain lions, wood rats, vultures (VUL-cherz), songbirds, snakes, and lizards.

IT'S A FACT

Desert squirrels hibernate. They take a long sleep, right through the hottest part of summer.

▲ The wood rat or pack rat gathers shiny materials, twigs, and dirt. It builds a home, or mound, that it can move in and out of. Its home is called a midden.

11

Plains and Wetlands

These windy, dry places look like seas of grass. Summers are hot. Winters are cold. There are few trees, but many animals. Some are antelopes (AN-teh-lopes), bison, wolves, rabbits, prairie dogs, foxes, skunks, mice, owls, toads, snakes, and loads of insects.

prairie dogs

Many animals that live here have colors that blend with the grasses. Since those animals are well hidden, their **predators** (PREH-duh-terz) have a hard time spotting them.

◀ bull snake

Wetlands are areas that stay wet and warm all year. They are filled with trees and vines and moss. Animals that live here are panthers, deer, skunks, alligators, crocodiles, turtles, and wading birds such as storks and herons.

▲ Alligators' sharp teeth and strong jaws help them to catch and eat prey.

✓ POINT

Read More About It

Read more about animals that live near estuaries and some animals that live in the oceans. Share your findings with classmates.

WHAT'S AN ESTUARY?

An **estuary** (ES-chuh-wair-ee) is part of a river or stream that runs into the ocean. Estuaries have both freshwater and saltwater. They are important habitats with rich soil. They are safe places for fish to lay eggs. And there's lots of shellfish for birds to eat.

All Kinds of Animals

Picture this. You are on a nature walk. You see a frog jump over a log. You spot a bee buzzing near a flower. You brush against what looks like a twig. But it isn't. It's a walking stick bug, an insect that looks so much like a twig that you didn't notice it. And neither do its predators. What a great **adaptation** (a-dap-TAY-shun)! Some adaptations are physical (FIH-zih-kul). They involve animals' body parts, such as the legs on the walking stick or the structure of an animal's mouth.

▲ walking stick bug

Adaptations for Eating—Mouths of Yesterday and Today

- Fish that feed on the water's surface have mouths that turn up. Bottom-feeding fish have mouths that turn down.

- Meat-eating animals have sharp teeth to tear apart their food.

Bottom-feeding	Surface-feeding

Green sturgeon	Herring

Past	Present

T. Rex	Grizzly bear

Fast Movers

Some animals have body parts that help them to move fast.

the pronghorn

The pronghorn is the fastest mammal in North America. It can run up to 60 miles (97 kilometers) an hour for a short distance. It can run about 45 miles (72 kilometers) per hour for longer periods. Its heart, lungs, and windpipe are large. These help it to breathe while running.

☑ POINT

Talk About It

How do humans adapt to their environment?
Share your thoughts with a classmate.

• Many plant eaters have wide, flat teeth that grind up plants.

• Some animals eat both meat and plants. They have some sharp teeth and some flat teeth.

Past	Present		Past	Present

Stegosaurus	White-tailed deer		Didelphodon	Coyote

15

▲ bighorn sheep

Climbers

Some animals live on steep, rocky hills and mountains. Their hooves have sharp edges. They are shaped to hold on to rocky ground.

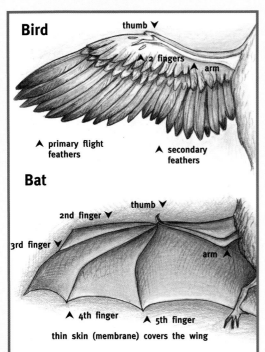

Bird

thumb ▼

▲ 2 fingers

▲ arm

▲ primary flight feathers

▲ secondary feathers

Bat

thumb ▼

2nd finger ▼

3rd finger ▼

arm ▲

▲ 4th finger

▲ 5th finger

thin skin (membrane) covers the wing

Flyers

Bats and most birds have strong, broad wings. Feathers help birds to fly, float, and stay warm and dry. Yet feathers are almost weightless. Bird and bat bones, too, weigh almost nothing. The less a bird or bat weighs, the easier it is for it to fly.

Birds Big and Small

Whooping cranes have long beaks. Their long legs help them wade in water to find food. Whooping cranes are the tallest birds in North America. They can grow to be 5 feet (1.52 meters) tall. Yet they weigh just 15 or 16 pounds (7.3 kilograms)!

The smallest birds in North America are hummingbirds. They hover in midair while drinking from flowers. Some hummingbirds are just 3 inches (7.6 centimeters) tall.

hummingbird ▲

They Made a Difference

John James Audubon, 1785–1851

This American artist studied birds. His book *The Birds of America* shows, up close, what different birds look like. It tells how different birds live.

▼ *Least Bittern* by Audubon

4 SOLVE THIS

What is the height difference in inches between the tallest bird and the smallest?

a. 57 inches
b. 70 inches
c. 15 inches

✓ Math Point

What steps did you use to solve the problem?

It's Nature's Way

Animals act by **instinct** (IN-stingkt). This means they just do something. They haven't learned it. They don't think about it.

Hibernation (hy-ber NAY-shun) and **migration** (my-GRAY-shun) are two different instincts. Swimming is another. No one teaches a fish to swim. It just swims. No one teaches schools of fish or flocks of birds to stay together. They just do.

It's instinct: Spiders weave ▶ webs. Beavers build lodges. Ducks fly in a V formation.

An Instinct to Work Together

Honeybees work together by instinct. The queen lays all the eggs for the hive. The drones are males that mate with the queen. The worker bees guard the hive. They flap their wings to keep it cool. They collect nectar (NEK-ter), the sweet juice that some plants make. Honeybees make both the honeycombs and the honey.

5 SOLVE THIS

A queen bee can lay about 1,500 eggs in one 24-hour period. About how many eggs can she lay in one week?

✓ Math Point

How did you check your work?

CAREERS IN SCIENCE

A person who works with insects is an entomologist (en-toh-MAH-luh-jist). This scientist studies insect life cycles and insect habitats. A love of nature and science are the best places to start. An entomologist might work in a museum, or outdoors where insects live.

19

Long-Distance Flyers

Each fall Monarch butterflies migrate (MY-grate) south from their homes in Canada and the northern United States. They go to Mexico, California, and other places. In the spring, they take the same long trip back home.

IT'S A FACT

Some of what animals do is not instinct. It is learned. A young seagull watches its mother smash a clamshell on a rock and eat the clam. The baby gull learns how to feed itself.

6 SOLVE THIS

MONARCH BUTTERFLY FALL MIGRATION MAP

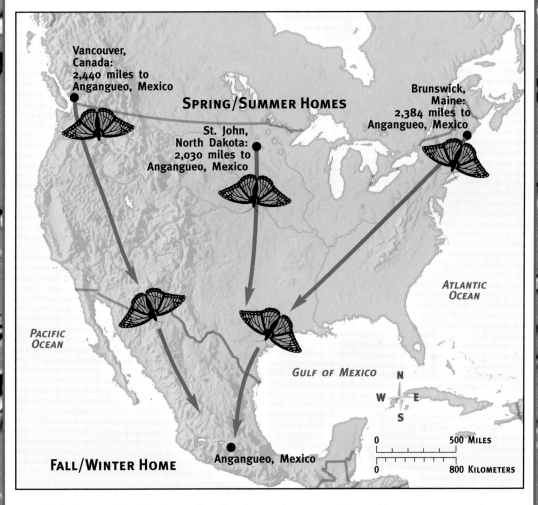

Vancouver,
Canada:
2,440 miles to
Angangueo, Mexico

SPRING/SUMMER HOMES

St. John,
North Dakota:
2,030 miles to
Angangueo, Mexico

Brunswick,
Maine:
2,384 miles to
Angangueo, Mexico

PACIFIC
OCEAN

ATLANTIC
OCEAN

GULF OF MEXICO

N
W   E
S

0   500 MILES

0   800 KILOMETERS

FALL/WINTER HOME   Angangueo, Mexico

Which butterfly had to fly farther, the one from Vancouver or the
one from Brunswick? How much farther?

 **Math Point**

What strategy did you use to solve this problem?

Changing Habitats

▲ Everglade kite

The Everglade kite is a bird that is native to Florida. Its only food is a native snail called the apple snail. Scientists think someone placed a different kind of snail into the apple snails' habitat. The new snail took over. Now the apple snails are dying out.

The kite's beak cannot grab onto the other snail. Now the Everglade kite is in danger of becoming extinct.

Placing one animal species into another's habitat is one way people change an animal's habitat.

What Nature Does to Habitats

Nature changes habitats. A volcano eruption may form an island, a mountain, or destroy a forest. Earthquakes and other natural disasters change landscapes, too. Melting glaciers can change the course of a river or carve a new one.

The dinosaurs died out because of natural causes. Many scientists think a huge asteroid (AS-tuh-roid) hit Earth. The crash spread dust around the whole planet and changed Earth's climate. All of the natural changes have affected animals over time. But humans are the biggest reason why animals are in danger today.

An artist's conception ▼ of an asteroid striking Earth.

◀ This *Tyrannosaurus rex* skeleton was found in 2000 in North Dakota. Her name is Sue.

▲ cockroach

Some Animals Survive

Some animals move away to find new homes when their habitat changes. They are able to get the food, water, air, and shelter they need in a different place. Other animals survive because they are faster or stronger than the other species around them.

THE COCKROACH

Cockroaches have hardly changed in 300 million years. Why? Cockroaches have unusually good adaptations:

- They eat almost anything.
- They are hard to crush.
- They are fast runners.
- Tiny hairs on their tail ends warn them of danger. They start running to safety in one hundredth of a second!
- They can even live for days with no heads.

▲ Many experts believe that the cockroach is as old as the dinosaurs.

▲ The bald eagle was once nearly extinct. It was listed as an endangered animal in 1967. Since then, more have been counted every year. It was taken off the endangered list in 1999.

7 SOLVE THIS

a. How many nesting pairs of eagles were in the lower forty-eight states in 1981?
b. How many pairs in 2000?
c. What is the difference between the two numbers?

✓ Math Point

Do your answers seem reasonable?

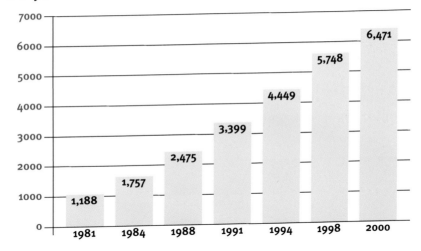

25

Some Animals Don't Survive

Some animals have trouble surviving. They may become endangered (in-DANE-jerd) or even extinct.

The Passenger Pigeon

There were once about four billion passenger pigeons in North America. People hunted them, and turned their forest habitat into farmland. The last passenger pigeon died at the Cincinnati Zoo in 1914. Her name was Martha.

8 **SOLVE THIS**

You've read that there were once about four billion passenger pigeons in North America. Cockroaches have been the same for 300 million years. Write out each number in numerals, with commas in the correct places.

✔ **Math Point**

How could you check your work?

▲ passenger pigeon

26

Everyday SCIENCE

You can help endangered animals by not wasting resources such as freshwater and paper. You can make sure to put out any campfires. The more we leave natural resources untouched in the wild, the better for the animals.

The golden bear of California has been extinct in the wild since 1922. A few still live in zoos. ▼

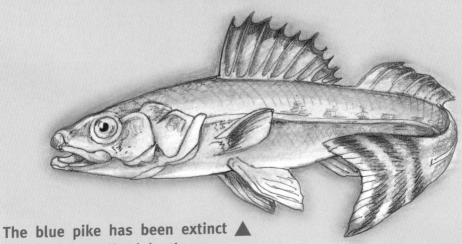

The blue pike has been extinct ▲ since 1983. It lived in the Great Lakes in the United States and Canada.

27

Conclusion

Maybe dinosaurs once lived in your backyard, but we know they don't now. They died out millions of years ago. North America is a very different place than it was back then. The climate is colder and wetter now. But there still are forests, deserts, and many other habitats for animals to live and to thrive in.

North American Animal

248 million years ago

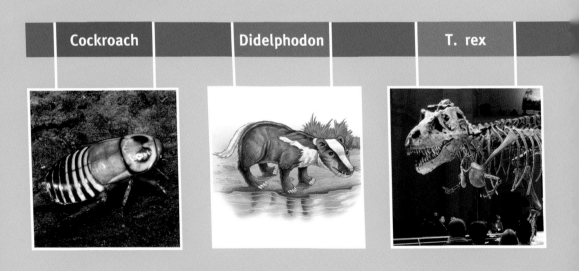

| Cockroach | Didelphodon | T. rex |

We also know that North American habitats are always changing. Some changes are caused by nature, but many are caused by humans.

People are learning more about animals and their habitats. Scientists work to teach people what animals need to survive and to be taken off the endangered species list. There are laws to protect animals. There are zoos and nature preserves to help keep them safe. So, there is hope for the animals in North America. Maybe they will be around millions of years from now.

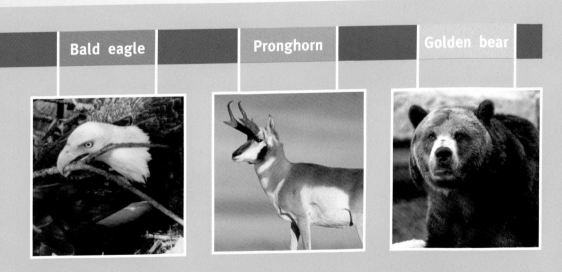

of the Past and Present

65 million years ago	12 thousand years ago

Bald eagle · Pronghorn · Golden bear

SOLVE THIS ANSWERS

1. Page 4

a. Evergreen forest is the biggest habitat.

b. Chaparral is the smallest.

c. The tundra and polar desert habitat and the desert and semidesert habitat are farthest from each other.

Math Checkpoint

a. and b. Measure each habitat on the map at its widest and tallest points.

c. Measure the closest points of each possible pair of habitats.

2. Page 6

105 miles (168 kilometers)

Math Checkpoint

Estimating helps. You can use mental math:

10 x 7 = 70 (20 x 7 = 140)

5 x 7 = 35 (4 x 7 = 28)

70 + 35 = 105 (140 + 28 = 168)

3. Page 10

73° to 93°F

Math Checkpoint

You need the daytime temperature and the two numbers that tell the range.

4. Page 17

a. 57 inches

Math Checkpoint

To find the answer, subtract the smallest bird (3 inches) from the tallest bird (60 inches).

60 − 3 = 57.

5. Page 19

10,500 eggs in a week. 1,500 x 7 = 10,500

Math Checkpoint

To check your work, divide 10,500 by 7 to get 1,500.

6. Page 21

The butterfly from Vancouver had to travel 56 miles farther.

Math Checkpoint

To find the answer, locate how far the butterfly from Vancouver traveled (2,440 miles) and subtract how far the butterfly from Brunswick traveled (2,384 miles).

7. Page 25

a. 1,188

b. 6,471

c. 6471 − 1188 = 5,283

Math Checkpoint

a. and b. To find the first two answers, look information up on the chart.

c. The answer is reasonable if it's about 1,000 less than 6,471.

8. Page 26

a. 4,000,000,000

b. 300,000,000

Math Checkpoint

To check answers, figure out how many zero placeholders you need to write for each number.

Glossary

adaptation	(a-dap-TAY-shun) a behavior and/or body feature that helps animals or plants live in a certain place in nature (page 14)
camouflage	(KA-muh-flahj) coloring or patterning that helps the wearer blend with its environment (page 7)
continent	(KAHN-tih-nent) any one of seven large areas that make up the land on Earth (page 4)
equator	(ih-KWAY-ter) an imaginary line around the middle of Earth which divides it into north and south parts (page 4)
estuary	(ES-chuh-wair-ee) the part of a river or stream that flows into an ocean (page 13)
extinct	(ik-STINGKT) died out completely; no longer anywhere on Earth (page 3)
habitat	(HA-bih-tat) a place in nature where certain animals and plants live; each habitat has its own kind of climate and land or water conditions (page 2)
hibernate	(HY-ber-nate) to be asleep or at rest for a long period of time (page 8)
instinct	(IN-stingkt) a behavior that is not learned (page 18)
migration	(my-GRAY-shun) to move as a group from one place to another (page 18)
nocturnal	(nahk-TER-nul) happening at night; animals that are active after sunset are nocturnal (page 11)
predator	(PREH-duh-ter) an animal that survives by hunting and eating other animals (page 12)
species	(SPEE-sheez) a certain kind of animal or plant (page 2)
survive	(ser-VIVE) to stay alive (page 2)

Index

adaptation, 14, 24
alligators, 13
Apatosaurus, 3
arctic fox, 7
armadillos, 10
Audubon, John James, 17
bats, 16
bears, 6, 8, 27
bighorn sheep, 10
birds, 2, 11, 13, 16–18, 22
camouflage, 7
chaparral, 11
cockroach, 24
continent, 4
deserts, 4–5, 10–11, 28
endangered animals, 26–27, 29
equator, 4
estuary, 13
evergreen forests, 8
extinct, 3
forests, 3–4, 8, 22, 28
freshwater, 13
grasslands, 4–5
habitats, 2–5, 13, 28–29
hibernate, 8, 11
hibernation, 18
honeybees, 19
hummingbirds, 17
instinct, 18–20
jack rabbit, 10
learned behavior, 20
migration, 18
Monarch butterflies, 20–21
nocturnal, 11

passenger pigeons, 26
physical adaptations, 14
polar desert, 5
prairies, 4
predators, 12
pronghorn, 15
saltwater, 13
seagull, 20
species, 2, 29
squirrels, 11
subtropical forests, 5
Sue the dinosaur, 23
survive, 2, 29
teeth, 13
tundra, 5
turtles, 13
walking stick bug, 14
whooping crane, 17, 19
wings, 16
woolly mammoth, 7